Golf Jokes

Golf Jokes

350 HILARIOUS QUIPS, ZINGERS, AND BELLY LAUGHS

JOSHUA SHIFRIN

Skyhorse Publishing

Skyhorse Publishing books may be purchased in bulk at special discounts for sales promotion, corporate gifts, fund-raising, or educational purposes. Special editions can also be created to specifications. For details, contact the Special Sales Department, Skyhorse Publishing, 307 West 36th Street, 11th Floor, New York, NY 10018 or info@skyhorsepublishing.com.

Skyhorse® and Skyhorse Publishing® are registered trademarks of Skyhorse Publishing, Inc.®, a Delaware corporation.

Visit our website at www.skyhorsepublishing.com.

10 9 8 7 6 5 4 3 2

Library of Congress Cataloging-in-Publication Data is available on file.

Cover design by Kai Texel
Cover illustration by Ian Baker
Interior images by Ian Baker

ISBN: 978-1-5107-6704-1
Ebook ISBN: 978-1-5107-6705-8

Printed in China

Table of Contents

Introduction

Isn't golf just the best game? I'm guessing that if you're reading this book, you likely agree. The thrill starts early in the week as I anticipate my weekend round. As the weekdays mercifully inch toward pay dirt, I can almost feel the excitement of the first tee. I've played countless rounds, yet the night before I meet up with my foursome, there are times I can barely sleep. I just lie in bed, thinking about how I am going to grip and rip my drive right down the first fairway. My irons are crisp, my short game is perfection, and I'm surgically carving up the greens as I drain one putt after another. With my head heavy from a week of exhaustion, my heart is nevertheless pounding as I add up my ideal score card. Could it be? Is it possible? YES! I've finally broken 70! As my comrades toast me at the 19th hole, I can almost taste how smooth my brewsky feels as it slides down my throat and I bask in my sheer domination and mastery of the game I love.

As I step into the first tee box with my dreams from merely hours earlier still dancing around in my subconscious, the inevitable, of course, happens. I stand with supreme confidence over that little dimpled white sphere and summarily slice my drive so severely that I could make the local butcher envious. And then it hits me like a four-iron to the noggin . . . DAMN, golf is a difficult game!

I now have two options. Either give up this masochistic endeavor—never!—or go see my local shrink and discuss my woes at $250 an hour. As neither option sounds viable, I use the next best recourse. I laugh away my ineptitude. As any good doctor might tell me, "Laughter is the best medicine." With this aphorism often apropos before I make the turn to the back nine, my fellow weekend warriors and I often search for the best quip to turn that snowman on the scorecard from tears of sorrow to tears of laughter.

With the aforementioned in mind, I have put together a list of the funniest, most humorous, side-stitching, belly-busting, toe-tickling (pick your preferred cliché) list of comedic prose to keep you laughing throughout anything this amazing game can throw at you.

Without further ado, I give you *Golf Jokes*.

Golfer's Glossary

Golf: An endless sequence of tragedies interrupted by the occasional miracle followed by a cold beer.

Oxymoron: An easy hole.

Politically correct: Golfers don't have "handicaps"; they're "stroke-challenged."

Golf etiquette: Always concede the fourth shot.

Mulligan: The reason golf balls come three to a sleeve.

Practice Tee: The place where most golfers go to adjust their severe slice into an even more severe hook.

> *"Golf is a good walk spoiled."*
> *—Mark Twain*

Handicapped golfer: A golfer who plays with his or her boss.

Male golfer: A confused soul who most often talks about women while playing golf and speaks of golf when he's with a woman.

Mulligan: The aspiration to hit a second poor shot in a row.

Golf's law: There is a direct correlation between the number of people watching you golf and the likelihood that you'll duff your next shot.

Fairway: A long piece of finely mowed grass running from the tee to the green normally found with a ball immediately to the left or right of it.

Gimme: An agreement between two poor putters.

"I have a tip that can take five strokes off anyone's game. It's called an eraser."
—Arnold Palmer

Just Putting Around . . .

I'm not really a bad putter; I just can't catch a break.

At the club championships, a man has a two-foot putt to win the tournament. When asked if it was a gimme, his playing partner informs him that he would have to hole it out. "You know," says the man, "a true gentleman would have conceded the putt." "That may be true," comes the retort, "but I'm not a gentleman today . . . I'm a golfer."

How do golfers procrastinate at work? They putter around.

A professor was taking his first golf lesson. When they got to the green, the professor asked the pro, "Is the word *P-U-T* or *P-U-T-T*?" The professional calmly explained, "The word is *P-U-T-T*. You see," he explained, "to *P-U-T* is to place something where you want it to go. To *P-U-T-T* is a hopeless effort to do the same thing."

The experienced golfers don't miss putts . . . they get robbed.

A poor golfer is once again having a terrible round. After many trips to the woods, digging up the course with his iron play, and too many putts to count, he is frustrated beyond words. "What do you think I should do?" he asks his caddie. "I'd say take your mind off of the game and don't play for a month." "What should I do after that?" the man asks expectantly. "Then I'd give up the game for good."

> *"The only sure rule in golf is he who has the fastest golf cart never has to play the bad lie."*
> **—Mickey Mantle**

"I didn't miss the putt. The stupid ball missed the hole."

A golfer was having a very difficult round. And despite the best efforts of the player and the caddie, things didn't get better. The player was all over the course. In and out of the woods. He struggled in the traps and three- and four-putted almost every hole. At the end of the round, the player looked at the caddie and said, "What do I owe you?" "The first thing you owe me," the exhausted caddie responded, "is an apology."

A man and his friend were playing a leisurely round when a single behind them seemed to be playing very quickly. As the twosome finished the front nine and headed for the 10th tee, they looked back to see the woman putting quickly and then rushing toward them. Finally, one of the men said, "Would you like to play through?" "That would be great," the exasperated woman said. "My husband was involved in a terrible accident, and I need to get home as soon as possible."

A golfer was having a particularly bad round. She couldn't get off of the tee. Her divots were going farther than her shots off the fairway. She was spending so much time in the traps that she might as well have spent the day at the beach. And a three-putt on the green was a welcome surprise. As the player mercifully walked up the 18th fairway, she stopped at the water hazard right in front of the green, looked at her caddie, and somberly stated, "I think I'm going to drown myself in this pond," to which the caddie responded, "I doubt you could keep your head down for that long."

It takes real inner strength to keep it together when lining up your fourth putt.

> *"We learn so many*
> *things from golf—*
> *how to suffer, for instance."*
> *—Bruce Lansky*

A man shows up to his regular golf game with a huge gorilla. At first, the friends are worried. But when the man explains that the gorilla is well trained and is an excellent golfer, they are all intrigued. And sure enough, on the par-4 first hole, the gorilla hits a 450-yard drive that lands right in the middle of the green. "That's amazing!" one friend says. Another friend offers, "We should sign the gorilla up for the PGA Tour." And just as the men are counting their soon-to-be fortune, the gorilla stands over his 6-foot putt, reads the green carefully, and proceeds to hit his putt 450 yards.

To line up a two-foot putt, you should always aim two inches to the left of the right edge.

A husband and wife were playing in their club's mixed four-somes. The wife got on the tee and knocked her drive straight down the middle of the fairway. Her husband proceeded to slice the next shot right behind a big tree. Undeterred, his better half hooked her next shot around the tee, and the ball settled a foot from the pin. Per his MO, the husband pushed the putt eight feet past the hole. Thankfully, his wife calmly drained the eight-footer. As the couple walked to the next hole, the wife said, "We need to step it up. That was a bogey five." "Don't blame me," the husband snapped, "I only took two of those shots."

Player: "Left edge?" Caddie: "I'm not sure. I generally don't read putts for a quadruple bogey."

A struggling golfer was having the worst round of his life. He couldn't get off of the tee, his iron game was in shambles, and he was 20 over par after the front nine. Things unfortunately didn't get much better, and as the futility continued, the golfer began to steam. Finally, mercifully, the round was coming to an end. But when the exasperated golfer missed a 3-foot putt on the 18th, he couldn't take it any longer. Looking directly at his caddie, he screamed, "You've got to be the worst caddie in the world!" The caddie looked directly at the golfer and without missing a beat said, "I doubt it. That would just be too much of a coincidence."

Golfer: "Your read on that putt was awful." Caddie: "That may be true, but at least you had the correct club."

> *"I know I am getting better at golf because I am hitting fewer spectators."*
> —Gerald Ford

John Smith was a fanatical golfer. He was out with his caddie when they came to the first green. The golfer got on his hands and knees and carefully inspected the putting surface. He then cleared off all of the debris on and around the hole. He held a wet finger in the air to assess the wind. Not yet ready to putt, he turned to his caddie and asked, "Was this green mowed this morning?" "Yes, Mr. Smith." "From left to right or right to left?" "From left to right, Mr. Smith" came the caddie's reply. Finally, the golfer stood over the ball, putted, and missed the hole by four inches. He spun around, looked at his caddie, and said, "What time was it cut?"

If your best moments on the course are the practice swings and gimme putts, you might want to reconsider the game of golf.

A married couple is on the putting green on the 7th hole when the wife falls to the ground. "I think I'm having a heart attack," the woman groans. "Don't worry, honey," the man yells, "I'll go find some help." A few minutes later, the husband returns and begins to line up his putt. "I can't believe you're actually going to continue playing while I'm lying here dying," the incredulous woman says. "Not to worry," comes the retort. "I found a cardiologist on the 2nd hole, and he's going to help you." "Well, where in the world is he?" the sickly woman bellows. "He'll be here really soon," the man says calmly. "Everybody has already agreed to let him play through."

Golf can be so frustrating. On any given day you can slice, hook, shank, and four-putt every hole. And then, on the very next day, for no apparent reason, you play terribly.

A rabbi was playing golf with one of his congregants. On the 4th hole, the rabbi missed a two-foot putt and said, "Hoover." Later in the round, on the 9th hole, the rabbi hit his tee shot out of bounds and was heard again saying, "Hoover." And finally, after the round was over, the rabbi was adding up his poor performance on his score-card when he once again said, "Hoover!" The rabbi's playing partner was now more than curious and asked, "Excuse me, rabbi. I couldn't help but notice that every time things went awry you would say, 'Hoover.' What does that mean?" "Well, being a man of the cloth I don't like to swear, and 'Hoover' is the biggest damn I know."

If you took Latin in high school, then you surely learned about *caveat emptor*—"let the buyer beware." Be sure to remember this when buying a putter. Always remember to test out how far you can throw your putter before purchasing it.

> *"Golf appeals to the idiot in us and the child. Just how childlike golf players become is proven by their frequent inability to count past five."*
> —John Updike

An arrogant golfer and his caddie were about to tee off on a long par 3. The player looked at the caddie and said, "This should be as simple as a five wood and a putt." The caddie then suggested a more

conservative route and recommended a four iron and a wedge. The irate golfer chastised his caddie and said, "How dare you underestimate me. You should have figured out by now that I'm an excellent player." The caddie reluctantly gave the man his five wood and watched as he proceeded to top the tee shot and continued to gaze as it rolled about 20 yards down the fairway. Without missing a beat, the caddie then handed him his putter and said, "I can't wait to see this incredible putt."

As Ellen continued to give her husband golf advice, he had finally had enough. "I can't take it anymore!" the man cried. "If you say one more word, you'll drive me insane." "Okay, okay," his wife conceded, "But that's not a drive; it's a three-foot putt."

A golfer is having the round of his life. He's consistently driving the ball down the middle of the fairway. His iron play is superb. And his putter is on fire. For the first time in his life, he might actually break par as he stands on the 18th tee. As the weight of the moment hits him, he literally starts to shake. He proceeds to hook his tee shot into the woods. The man then duffs the next several shots and closes with a four-putt to blow the round. The frustrated man looks to his caddie and says, "What do you think about that finish?" To which the caddie replies, "I was about to call 9-1-1." "Why would you do that?" the curious golfer asks. "Because it's been years since I've seen a man choke like that."

A mixed foursome is out on the 13th green when a slight drizzle occurs. One of the husbands states, "A little rain doesn't bother us, does it, beautiful?" The other woman looks to his wife and says, "Why is he telling you not to let the rain bother you?" "He's not talking to me." The woman replies, "He's talking to his putter."

Half of the game of golf is fun and exciting; the other half is played on the green.

An elderly golfer set a goal to break 100 by the end of the summer. He was so determined that he promised his caddie a large cash reward if he could help him achieve his objective. As the months wore on, there were several close calls, but victory was yet to be obtained. Finally, on one of the last days of summer, victory was in sight. The older gentleman was on the green, about eight feet from the hole, and sitting with a current score of 97. The two men were giddy with excitement when the golfer nervously sent his putt ten feet past the hole. Without missing a beat, the caddie quickly picked up that ball and said, "Congratulations! You've shot a 99. Anyone in their right mind can see that this last putt was a gimme."

> *"Golf is a game in which you yell fore, shoot six, and write down five."*
> *—Paul Harvey*

Two golfers are on the fourth green when the first player four-putts. He looks to his friend and says, "I'm afraid old age has caught up with me. I clearly have a case of the yips." His friend laughs and says, "Yips . . . shmips. You're 26 years old. Perhaps it has something to do with the six beers you've had since we've teed off."

John brings his friend Alan to join his weekly golf game. When the regulars ask if the friend is any good, John replies, "He's excellent." However, when Alan slices his first drive into the woods, the regulars say, "We thought you said he was good." "Just continue to watch," comes the reply. The golfer goes into the woods, hooks his next shot around a tree onto the green, and proceeds to make the putt for birdie. However, on the very next hole, Alan drives his tee shot right into a lake. "We thought you said he was a good golfer?," comes the outcry. "Just wait," John responds. The regulars watch as Alan takes off his clothes all the way down to his underwear and submerges himself into the middle of the lake. After staying underwater for three minutes, the worried group finally sees Alan's hand emerge. "He's drowning and needs help," one of the regulars yells. "Not at all," John says calmly. He's just asking for his pitching wedge."

Two golfers are both dealing with a lot of stress in their personal life. The first golfer mentions to the second that his therapist suggested that he play golf with an imaginary ball. They agree that the advice couldn't hurt. So when they meet for their weekend game together, they both tee up an imaginary ball, take their respective swings, and note that their drives went long and straight down the middle of the fairway. As the imaginary round progresses, both golfers are ecstatic with their sub-par rounds. When they get to the par-3 eighteenth hole, the score is tied, and they can feel their stress easing. The first golfer takes out a six iron and reports that his drive landed softly on the edge of the green. The second golfer responds in the same manner and says his ball was right next to his partner's. The first golfer stands over his imaginary putt, takes his swing, and reports that his 15-footer just dropped into the bottom of the cup. The second golfer smiles and says, "Sorry to tell you this, but you just hit my ball."

A man is in a confessional when he begins, "Forgive me father, for I have sinned. I used some terrible language while playing golf yesterday." "Tell me what happened, my son," the priest says." "I was out on the course when I hit a terrific drive right now in the middle of the fairway. I was so excited until the ball hit a telephone line in midflight and fell straight to the ground." "And that's when you used the foul language?" asks the priest. "No, father," says the man. "After that, a squirrel came out of the woods, grabbed my ball, and started to run away." "And that's when you used the inappropriate language?" the clergyman asks. "No father, because after that, an eagle swooped down and picked up the squirrel in his talons and started to fly away." "Is that when you used the bad language?" "Not yet, father. After that the eagle flew over some woods and dropped the ball." "So that's when you swore?" the priest asks now somewhat exasperated. "No father, because when the ball came down it hit a branch, the bounced off of a big rock, shot toward the green, and settled six inches from the hole." "That's quite a story," the priest says. "But I still don't understand why you used the foul language." "Because I missed the damn putt."

The Weekend Warrior

For some, it's not a sin to play golf on Sundays . . . it's a crime.

A man was an enthusiastic golfer but unfortunately wasn't very good. On one beautiful Saturday afternoon, he walked through his front door and proclaimed to his wife, "I scored a 128 today." "That's great!" his supportive wife said, "Your golf game is improving." "Thanks," the husband said, "But I was bowling."

> *"If you drink, don't drive.*
> *Don't even putt."*
> *—Dean Martin*

Where can you find a golfer on most Saturday nights? Out clubbing, of course.

A man was working in his office supply store when the secretary told him he had an angry customer on line two. However, when he picked up the phone, he was surprised to hear the angry man was Father Mulchahy from the local church. The priest began by saying, "I'm very upset about the pencils we ordered." "What's the problem?" the man inquired. "Didn't you receive them?" "Oh, we received them," the priest said, "but they were golf pencils, and each was stamped with the words "Play Golf On Sundays."

Golf is the perfect thing to do on a Sunday because there is a lot of praying involved.

On a crisp Sunday morning, Ralph showed up late to his tee time. His playing partners were somewhat perturbed and asked why he was running behind. "Well," John explained, "It's Sunday and I was feeling guilty about missing church, so I decided to leave it up to chance and flip a coin." "That doesn't explain why you are so late," his annoyed friends answered. Ralph looked at his foursome sheepishly and responded, "The good Lord must have really wanted me to go to church because I had to flip the coin twenty times."

In the United States, many of us bow our heads in church on Sundays; the rest do it on the golf course.

A priest decides to call in sick and skip church on Sunday in order to play a round of golf. As the priest is about to tee off, an angel in heaven asks God, "Are you going to let this man of the cloth get away with this?" "Of course not," God says, "Just keep watching." However, just moments later, the priest hits a booming tee shot that bounces off of a rock, then a tree, only to land on the green and roll slowly into the cup for a hole in one. "Why would you let him do that?" the astounded angel asks. God laughs and says, "Just think about it. Who is he going to be able to tell?"

> *"You don't know what pressure is until you play for five bucks with only two bucks in your pocket."*
> —Lee Trevino

Golfer: "Do you think it's a sin to play golf on Sunday?" Priest: "The way you play, I'd say it's a sin on any day."

George was a crazed golf enthusiast who ate, drank, and slept golf. On one fateful Saturday, he was having an exceptionally good round when some storm clouds rolled in. George refused to leave the round of his life when he was struck by lightning and died instantly. When he got to heaven, St. Peter was there waiting. "George" he began, "you have lived a good life and now you will live eternally in the paradise of heaven where you can play as much golf as you wish."

But George could only weep tears of sorrow. "What is it?" St. Peter asked, "Will you miss your family?" George could only shake his head no. "Will you miss your friends?" "No," George whimpered. "Is it your successful career?" "That's not it, either," George wailed. "Then why are you so upset?" St. Peter asked. "I think I left my lucky six-iron on the 12th hole."

The Caddie Said . . .

Golfer: "Golf is a funny game". Caddie: "It is when *you* play it."

At Waterville in Ireland, a golfer is having a fabulous round when he hits a shot into the tall grass. Not wanting to take the penalty, he looks to his experienced caddie and says, "Do you think we have a chance of finding it?" To which the caddie responds, "If that ball was wrapped in bacon, a bloodhound couldn't find it."

The only truly honest golfers are the ones who always use a caddie.

A man is playing his round with an insubordinate young caddie. After numerous rude comments from the employee, the golfer has had enough. "As soon as we finish up, I'm going to report you to your boss. What do you think about that?" the angry golfer asks. "Oh no," comes the sarcastic response, "But at the rate you play, by the time we finish, I'll be ready to retire."

> *"I started watching golf for the first time yesterday. I'm really worried about myself. I was actually enjoying it."*
> —Ewan McGregor

Golfer: "This golf course is terrible!" Caddie: "We left the golf course 45 minutes ago."

A golfer was in a real pickle when his ball went into the woods and got stuck in a tree branch. The perplexed player thought for a while and then looked to his caddie for assistance. "Any idea what type of shot I should take?" the man asked. "I have just the right shot for you," the caddie stated as he reached into his bag and handed the man a flask full of alcohol.

I had to get a new caddie at the turn. My first one had a stomach-ache from laughing too hard.

A nervous caddie came running into the pro shop and exclaimed, "Mrs. Jones was just stung by a bee, and she's feeling faint. What should I do?" "Where was she stung?' the golf pro inquired. "Between the fourth and fifth hole," came the nervous response. The pro thought for a second and then said, "If I've told her once, I've told her 100 times . . . her stance is too wide."

Golfer: "Do you think I can get home from here?" Caddie: "That all depends . . . how far away do you live?"

An impatient golfer was playing a round with her caddie when they came upon a group on the green ahead of them. "What do you suggest I do?" the woman inquired. "I'm ready to hit now." The caddie thought for a second and then replied, "Well, as I see it you have one of two options. You can shank it now. Or wait until they're off the green and then top it about 10 yards ahead of you."

> *"If you watch a game, it's fun.*
> *If you play at it, it's recreation.*
> *If you work at it, it's golf."*
> *—Bob Hope*

Golfer: "That was really bad slice." Caddie: "I wouldn't call that a slice. I'd call it half of the pie."

A golfer is debating his shot that is sitting perilously behind a tree. The player looks to his caddie for advice and asks, "Do you think I should go through the tree or around it?" The caddie assesses the situation and says, "I would go around it." The player, not yet convinced, replies with, "I thought trees were 90 percent air." "That's true," the caddie says, "but so is a screen door."

A golfer and his caddie are out on the course. The golfer, who is not very good, hits one errant shot after another. The caddie does his best to assist, but his client is a hopeless cause. After the round, the golfer looks at his caddie and says, "How do you like my game?" The caddie, who can't contain himself, looks the man directly in the eye and says, "Not bad, sir, but I personally prefer golf."

Golfer: "I've never played this poorly before." Caddie: "Wow . . . I didn't realize you've ever played before."

A golfer was out with his caddie, and he was struggling mightily. He was out of bounds, in the woods, and found every body of water. After a couple of hours, the caddie was exhausted. When the round was nearly at completion, the golfer was on the edge of a sand trap. "What club do you think I should use?" the golfer asked. "It depends," the caddie shot back, "What game are you trying to play?"

> *"I regard golf as an expensive*
> *way of playing marbles."*
> *—G.K. Chesterton*

Golfer: "Do you think I can carry that bunker?" Caddie: "It's got two tons of sand in it, so I really doubt it."

A man and his caddie have a 6 a.m. tee time. However, after numerous disasters, the morning round turns into the afternoon. Finally, on the 18th, they are nearing completion when the golfer hits yet another slice into the woods. The caddie finds the ball and alerts his golfer, who takes one look and says, "That can't be my ball. It's far too old." To which the caddie responds, "It's been a long time since we started."

Caddie: "That's what they call a son-in-law shot. It's not completely what you were hoping for, but you'll take it."

A notoriously cheap golfer was always looking to find a way to save money. So when he went to the caddie station, everyone was surprised. He approached the head caddie and said, "I need a caddie who is good at finding lost balls," to which the head caddie responded, "Frank has the best eyes on the staff. He seems to find every ball that's lost." "Great," replied the miser, "ask him to find me one so I can start my round."

A player looks at an unfamiliar hole and says, "What's beyond the green?" The caddie smiles and says, "Nothing but bogeys."

A poor player is taking out his frustrations on his caddie, blaming him for each and every poor shot. Finally, on the par-3 18th, the golfer chunks his shot, and it lands in a marsh fifty yards short of the green. He looks angrily at the caddie and says, "Why didn't you tell me that there was a marsh there?" The caddie, who has had enough abuse, replies, "I would have told you, but I didn't know you were planning on laying up on a par 3."

> *"It took me seventeen years to get three thousand hits in baseball. It took one afternoon on the golf course."*
> *—Hank Aaron*

Why is a golf cart, at times, preferable to a caddie? Because the cart won't laugh, made snide comments, or most importantly . . . count.

A golfer is having a terrible round and complains to his caddie, "I don't normally play this way." After a few more bad holes, the golfer reiterates, "I truly don't usually play this way." And finally, after the horrible round comes to a conclusion, the golfer apologizes again and says, "I don't know what happened today. But I never play this way." To which the caddie responds, "I understand. But I'm curious, what game do you usually play?"

Golfer: "Please stop looking at your yardage chart. I find it distracting." Caddie: "This is actually a map. I have no idea where we are."

A golfer is having a very bad round and is blaming everyone, and everything, but himself. At first he chalks up his ineptness to his poor equipment. As the round gets worse, he starts cursing the quality of the course. And finally, at the end of the round, the frustrated golfer looks at his caddie and says, "Why do you keep looking at your watch? It's very distracting!" To which the caddie replies, "It's actually not a watch . . . it's a compass."

After a poor round of golf, a defeated golfer looked at his caddie and said, "I would move both heaven and Earth to score in the 90s." The caddie smiled and said, "Next time you'd better try heaven. You moved a lot of earth today, and it clearly didn't help."

A golfer is playing a new course when he hooks a ball deep into the woods. The caddie suggests that he take a drop, but the man says he thinks they should look for it. "I've got eagle eyes," the golfer tells his caddie. "I bet I can find it." To which the caddie responds,

"You'll never find it. It landed in what we call 'Lion Country.'" "Why do they call it Lion Country," the man asks. "Because," explains the caddie, "if you find it, you're lion."

> *"There are two things you*
> *can do with your head down,*
> *play golf and pray."*
> *—Lee Trevino*

Nicole and Mary had just finished a less-than-stellar round when they were walking back to the clubhouse. Nicole looked at Mary and said, "What do you think I should give my caddie?" "I don't know about you," a frustrated Mary said, "but I'm planning on giving him my clubs!"

A golfer takes a mighty swing and slices his ball deep into the woods. His caddie suggests hitting another ball, but the golfer insists on finding the original. The caddie reluctantly agrees, and the two men go off in search of the errant shot. After ten minutes of futility, the caddie once again recommends playing a different ball, but the golfer is adamant that they keep searching. Finally, after another ten minutes, the caddie says, "I must insist that you take a drop." "I can't do that," the golfer says, "That's my lucky ball."

A very wealthy man shows up to his tee time with his caddie pulling a couch behind him. Incredulous, his playing partner says, "Are you really going to make your caddie lug that sofa all over the course after you?" "Of course not," The millionaire responded, "That's my psychiatrist."

An old caddie loved his job, but was growing increasingly weary of dealing with a couple of the regular hackers. On just such an occasion, as one of the caddie's regular inept clients was struggling through his round, the caddie didn't know how much more he could take. Finally, on the 18th hole, the golfer was about 140 yards from the green and turned to the exasperated caddie and said, "Do you think I can get there with a seven iron?" The caddie, who had had enough, looked the lost cause right in the eye and replied with one simple word: "Eventually."

A player is on the first tee, which is a par 3 with a water hazard in front of the hole. The caddie gives the man a new ball and stands back as the player tees up the ball. The golfer takes a few practice swings when the caddie stops him and says, "On second thought, perhaps you should hit a range ball."

A golfer is looking for just the right caddie. He approaches the caddie station and asks three different caddies to stand at attention. The man asks the first caddie, "What's 4 plus 4 plus 5?" to which the caddie responds, "13." "Very good," says the man. He asks the second caddie, "What's 3 plus 3 plus 4?" to which the caddie responds, "10." "Excellent," comes the reply. Finally, the golfer says to the third caddie, "You look like an ambitious young man. What's 4 plus 5 plus 6 plus 7?" The caddie looks pensive for a minute and then answers with, "Easy . . . it's 16." "You're hired!"

> *"Golf is the most fun*
> *you can have without*
> *taking your clothes off."*
> *—Chi Chi Rodriguez*

An elderly caddie has been working at his club for years. While he is beloved, he's clearly having trouble now with the physical nature of the job. Finally, the head pro approaches the aging caddie and says, "You've been working at this club for many years. Have you thought about retiring?" "I'd like to," comes the response, "but I need this job for the medical care." "You do realize that we don't offer health insurance to our caddies?" the pro says. "Oh, I know." says the caddie. "However, I figure that if I ever have a health emergency on the job, there will always be plenty of doctors around."

An older golfer was out with his caddie on a beautiful summer day. Unfortunately, the round was not going so well, as the hacker duffed shot after shot. Finally, when the day was mercifully coming to a conclusion, the golfer looked at his caddie in a self-loathing manner and proclaimed, "Surely I'm the worst player you've ever seen?" The empathetic caddie responded, "Don't be so hard on yourself. There are plenty worse than you." The golfer brightened and said, "Really? You're not just being nice?" To which the caddie replied, "No, it's true." The golfer, now enthused, said, "Maybe you could pair me up with them. It would be nice to play with someone on my level." The sheepish caddie then responded with, "I wish I could, but they all quit years ago."

A woman was playing a round of golf on a beautiful, but dangerous, course in Africa. The course was known to have wild animals, so the caddies all had to carry a rifle for extra protection. And sure enough, on the very first hole, a tiger jumped out onto the fairway. The caddie raised his rifle and shot it into the air, scaring the wild cat away. Then, on the ninth hole, a crocodile emerged from the water. Once again, a shot into the air scared the animal off. And as the round was coming to an end on the 18th, a huge leopard got close to the woman, but the caddie did nothing. As the fierce animal got closer, she began to run as the leopard took chase. The frantic golfer looked toward her caddie and yelled, "Help me!" to which the caddie calmly responded, "I'm sorry, ma'am, but you don't get a shot on this hole."

Fore!

How many golfers does it take to change a light bulb? Fore!

A golfer is on the 4th tee when he hits a terrible hook into the adjacent fairway. Unfortunately, it hits another golfer right in the head. The incensed victim screams, "You moron! I'm going to sue you for five million dollars." The golfer, now trying to do damage control, says, "I said 'fore.'" The injured player thinks for a second and then says, "I'll take it."

A priest was out enjoying a nice round of golf when, out of nowhere, he heard someone yell, "Fore!" Before he could react, the ball hit him right on top of the head. The golfer who hit the shot rushed to the scene and gushed his apology. The priest assured him

that he was fine. The man then smiled and said, "Well at least now I can tell all of my friends that I've finally hit my first holy one."

> "I can air mail the golf ball, but sometimes I don't put the right address on it."
> —Jim Dent

A poor golfer hit an errant tee shot. The ball hooked so badly that it ended up on an adjacent fairway, where it nearly missed another player. When the man who hit the wayward tee shot arrived at his ball, he was met by the irate player, who nearly avoided getting injured. "Your ball just missed me!" yelled the man. "I'm sorry," came the reply. "I didn't have time to yell 'Fore.'" "That's funny," the angry golfer said, "as you had plenty of time to yell out profanities."

Who's Keeping Score?

Two friends, Sylvia and Judy, are about to play a friendly round when Sylvia says, "Do you want to make it interesting and bet $5? Low score takes the cash." Judy agrees, and on the eighteenth Sylvia is ahead by one stroke when she slices her approach into the rough. Both women go searching for the ball, but neither can find it. Knowing that the two-stroke penalty will likely cost her the bet, Sylvia takes a ball out of her pocket and drops it on the fairway and pronounces that she found her errant shot. Judy, outraged, yells, "How dare you cheat me!" to which Sylvia, now incensed as well, replies, "What do you mean cheat? I found my ball." Judy, now even more agitated, responds, "And you're a liar, too!" "How can you be so sure?" Sylvia inquires. "Because I've been standing on your ball for the last ten minutes!"

If a golfer can't remember if he or she shot a 5 or 6 on a par 3, he or she most likely shot a 7.

Marc and Brian were fierce golfing rivals. With each always trying to get the upper hand, they watched each other like hawks. During one spirited round, Marc holed out on a par four and stated that he had scored a six. "Are you sure about that score?" Brian asked. "Oh, my mistake," Marc said, "I actually scored a five." "Your score was an eight," Brian retorted. "Impossible," Marc said. "How do you figure I got an eight?" "You said you shot a six, later changed it to a five, but in reality you shot a seven." "Then why did you say I scored an eight?" Marc asked. Brian said, "I'm assessing a one-stroke penalty for improving your lie."

> *"The loudest sound you hear is the guy jingling coins to distract a player he bet against."*
> *—Jim Murray*

I'm not saying Lisa is a cheater, but I once saw her hit a hole in one and mark it down as a zero.

An American went to Scotland to golf. He was paired up with a Scotsman, and on the very first hole the American hooked his drive deep into the woods. He immediately took a mulligan and drove it straight down the fairway. Happy with himself, the American asked his partner, "What do the Scottish call a mulligan?" "We call it a 3."

At a holiday party, two strangers struck up a conversation. After some small talk surrounding work and family, the subject of interests came up. The first woman said, "I'm an avid golfer. I play anytime I get the chance." To which the second woman responded, "I used to play, but I wasn't very good and eventually I gave it up." "You were really that bad?" the first woman inquired. "Yes. I used to score in the low seventies consistently." "Really?" the avid golfer responded somewhat impressed. "Really," the second woman admitted. "On nearly every hole."

How is fishing similar to golf? It helps to exaggerate.

An elderly couple is out on a new course. After hacking around for hours, they finally make their way to the clubhouse. After taking an exorbitant amount of time tallying up her scorecard, the wife looks at her husband and says, "What's par on this course?" "72," responds her husband. "Well I must be getting better," says the gleeful woman, "I was under par on almost every hole."

Why do doctors have a distinct advantage while playing golf? Because no one can read the writing on their scorecards.

> *"Golf is a game you play with your own worst enemy—yourself."*
> —Finley Peter Dunne

Hand positioning in golf is extremely important. Most "good" golfers use theirs to cover up their scorecards.

Two players were paired up for a round at their club. They met on the first hole and exchanged pleasantries. When they finally got around to golf, the first golfer asked, "So what's your handicap?" "Oh, I'm a scratch golfer," said the second. Obviously impressed, the first golfer said, "Wow . . . that's amazing." "It's really not that hard," the second responded, "I just write down all of my good scores and scratch out the bad ones."

You can improve your golf game in one of three ways. You can take the long-term approach and practice. You can take the expensive approach with lessons. Or you can use the easiest approach with an eraser.

Little girl: "My daddy is the best golfer. He gets to hit more shots than any of the other players."

If a golfer claims they never cheat, they are not only a cheater, but a liar, as well.

What's the easiest way to cut six strokes off of your score? Quit after the 17th hole.

> *"I regularly enjoy a round or two at my golf club. I sometimes play golf too."*
> *—Ronnie Barker*

Why is it that many golfers can't keep track of their daily finances but become Albert Einstein when adding up their scorecards?

A man comes home from an appointment with his physician and looks upset. "What happened?" his concerned wife asked. "Did the doctor give you bad news?" "The worst news," the despondent man said. "She told me I should give up golf." His wife, now a bit more relieved, asked, "Why, did she examine your back?" "No," the husband replied. "She examined my scorecard."

If at First You Don't Succeed . . .

In golf, it seems that the harder the player tries to make the shot just right before striking the ball, the less likely the golfer is to succeed in obtaining his or her objective.

Eugene's golf game is improving . . . he's getting much closer to the ball when he swings and misses than he used to.

When I hit the ball way to the left, it's a hook. When I hit the ball way to the right, it's a slice. And when I hit it right down the middle of the fairway, it's a miracle.

What is the easiest way to hook a ball into the woods? Try to slice it.

"*I'm convinced the reason most people play golf is to wear clothes they would not otherwise be caught dead in.*"
—*Roger Simon*

The best golfers hit the ball far, straight as an arrow, and infrequently.

What's the difference between a good and bad golfer? The good golfer addresses the ball before swinging. The poor golfer addresses the ball twice—once before swinging and once right after.

The only time it's truly too wet to play golf is when your cart capsizes.

Jim and Dan are playing a round when Jim hooks his drive deep into the woods. He looks to Dan and says, "Do you think we should go after it?" Dan thinks for a second and says, "Only if our golf cart has four-wheel drive."

Why is it so hard to hit a huge fairway and so easy to hit a very thin branch?

A dimwitted golfer goes to the pro shop and asks for colored golf balls. "I'm sorry," comes the reply. "We're all sold out. Would you like some white balls?" "No, thank you," the man responds. "They have to have color." "Do you mind if I ask why?" the employee asks. "Because if they have color they'll be easier to find in the sand traps."

> *"Golf is so popular simply because it is the best game in the world at which to be bad."*
> *—A. A. Milne*

I have no problem hitting the woods; I just really struggle to get out of them.

On a Monday morning at work, Maurice asked his coworker, "How was your weekend?" to which the coworker replied, "It was fantastic." "What made it so good?" Maurice inquired. "I put a bunch of hooks in the water." "Wow, I didn't know you were a fisherman." "Who said anything about fishing?" The coworker responded. "I was playing golf."

I'm not saying that he's an angry golfer, but after 18 holes, he broke 9 clubs.

An old man was talking to his son when his child inquired about his retirement in Florida. "It's going really well," his father said. "And I'm loving golf and am actually getting pretty good at it. I normally play in the mid-70s. If it's any hotter than that I would rather sit in the air conditioning."

The way many golfers play, they should put the flags on the greens at half-mast.

Alice Schwartz was known to be an avid golfer who could hold her own. However, everyone who knew her game well was also aware that she was terrible in the sand. While out with her playing partner, Alice hit a shot into a deep fairway bunker. "Which club do you think I should use?" Alice inquired. "Forget about the club," her partner retorted. "Just take plenty of food and water."

> *"Golf was my first glimpse of comedy. I was a caddie when I was a kid."*
> *—Bill Murray*

When your divot consistently goes farther than your ball, it's time to give up golf.

A woman is speaking with her friend on the first tee when she says, "I'm not sure if I want to hit a fade or a draw." She eventually steps up and hits her drive into the rough to the left of the fairway. "What happened?" inquires her friend. "Why do you ask?" comes the reply. "I clearly decided to hit a draw. If I wanted to hit a fade, I would have ended up in the rough to the right."

Why do golfers continue to keep buying golf balls? Because they're not very good swimmers.

Marco was a poor golfer but had a good attitude. One day, while playing with his friend, he continued to send the turf farther than the ball. "Oh my," Marco exclaimed, "the worms are going to think there is an earthquake today." To which his quick-witted friend responded, "Not to worry. The worms on this course are pretty smart. They're all probably just hiding under your golf ball for safety."

I once played a course that was so difficult I lost my first three balls in the ball washer.

Two friends went to play a new course that had a reputation for being very difficult. On the first hole, the first friend teed up his ball, took a mighty swing, and missed completely. He stepped away for a moment, then readdressed the ball. He took another huge swipe and missed again. Undeterred, he took one more attempt and barely made contact, sending the ball dribbling off of the tee. "Wow," the frustrated golfer said to his friend, "this really is a hard course."

> *"I was so bad at golf they would*
> *have to check me for ticks at*
> *the end of the round because I'd*
> *spent half the day in the woods."*
> *—Jeff Foxworthy*

It would be easier to keep your ball in the fairway if you golfers weren't so choosy about which fairway.

Susan, a young, vibrant woman, took a mighty tee shot on a par-5 and sliced the ball badly into the woods right behind a big tree. Undaunted, Susan took a bigger swipe, but unfortunately the ball struck a branch, shot straight back, and hit her in the head, instantly killing her. Moments later she found herself in front of the pearly gates, where St. Peter asked her, "I see you like to play golf. Are you any good?" "Well, I don't want to brag. But I got here in two."

The sand taunts you, the trees mock you, the water calls out to you, and yet golf is supposedly a quiet game.

Gene was known for his cheating on the course, and his playing partners were fed up. So when Gene was in a sand trap that was hidden from view, they were all listening intently as Gene hacked around for what seemed like an eternity. When he finally got his ball onto the green, his foursome asked, "How many shots was that?" "Two," Gene replied. "Oh come on," his frustrated compatriots yelled. "We heard at least four." "That's because it was a very deep trap, and two of the shots you heard were echoes."

It's a proven fact that an expensive golf ball is twice as likely to find the water as a range ball.

A couple of aliens from outer space were watching a golfer play a round. The golfer was struggling mightily. He was spraying the ball all over the course. He was in and out of the woods. He was often in the deep rough. The golfer often took several attempts to get out of the traps. The aliens correctly assumed that the human was playing some sort of strange game with a stick and a ball. Finally, the aliens watched as the ball disappeared into a hole. "Wow," one alien said to the other, "he's in real trouble now."

> *"My best score is 103, but I've only been playing for 15 years."*
> —*Alex Karras*

"I didn't lose my ball," the golfer quipped. "I know exactly where it is. It's right in the middle of the woods."

A man goes to a fortune teller who says, "I see a lot of water, trees, and sand. You're clearly going to be a golfer."

God and Moses are playing golf. God has a particularly long shot over the water when Moses says, "I'd lay up, God. That's a pretty long shot." To which God replies, "If Tiger Woods can do it, then so can I." God proceeds to hit his shot right into the middle of the lake to which he says, "No worries, I'll get it." God then walks to the lake, walks on top of the water, and retrieves his ball. A group of golfers behind them who witness the event come up to Moses and say, "Who does that guy think he is, Jesus Christ? "No," Moses responds. "He thinks he's Tiger Woods."

Why is it that when you tell yourself not to hit into the water the only word that reverberates through your head is *WATER*?

A young man and an older golfer went out for a round. On the very first hole, a par 3, there was a large water hazard right in front of the green. The old man took out a new sleeve of balls, teed up the first of them, and proceeded to promptly hit it right into the middle of the drink. He teed up another new ball, and then another and another, but each time the result was the same. Finally, he needed to pull out a new sleeve. The young golfer, somewhat perplexed, asked, "Why don't you use an old ball?" to which the older gentleman responded, "I've never had an old ball."

New golf balls are attracted to water. Plus, the strength of the attraction is in direct correlation to how expensive the balls are.

> *"The Statute of limitation on forgotten strokes is two holes."*
> *—Leslie Nielsen*

David and Michael are playing a delightful round of golf when Michael's errant shot goes deep down into a ravine and lands in some of the thickest rough either player has ever seen. Undeterred, Michael grabs an eight iron and goes searching for his ball. Incredibly, Michael finds a skeleton in the thick rough, holding onto an eight iron, with a ball right next to him. Michael, obviously shaken, yells to David to assist him. "Is everything okay?" David inquires. "It's fine," Michael responds. "But please get me my nine iron. Apparently you can't hit out of this with an eight."

Golfer #1: "Were you really under the whole day? "Golfer #2; "Yes . . . under a bush . . . under a tree . . . under a rock . . . and under the water!"

A poor golfer sliced a tee shot during his round and watched as it went into an open window. Assuming there was nothing he could do, he simply played on. At the end of his round a police officer was waiting for him. The officer said, "During your round, did you hit a ball through an open window?" "I did," the man answered honestly. "Well, when your ball shot into the house, it broke a mirror, scaring the family dog. The dog ran out of the house and into traffic, where he caused an accident. There are now three people in the hospital due to your errant shot." The golfer was horrified and said, "That's terrible. What can I do?" To which the officer answered, "Why don't you try closing up your stance?"

If your golf partner doesn't know the kind of trouble you are in, it's likely because they're stuck in a trap on the other side of the hole.

An elderly man was addressing his ball when an announcement came over the loudspeaker stating, "Will the gentleman on hole number one please refrain from hitting from the ladies' tee box?" The man stepped away, then readdressed the ball as the announcement came again, "Will the gentleman on hole number one please refrain from hitting from the ladies' tee box?" The man once again stepped away, regained his composure, and then readdressed his shot for a third time when the announcement came again, "Will the gentleman on hole number one please refrain from hitting from the ladies' tee box?" The old man, now clearly frustrated, looked toward the loudspeaker and yelled, "Will you please stop interrupting me and let me hit my second shot?"

Golf is a hard game to figure out. One day you'll be in the woods, sand, and water and the next day, for no reason at all, you'll be terrible.

> *"Most people play a fair game of golf, if you watch them."*
> *—Joey Adams*

Stuart was a terrible golfer. No matter how hard he tried, he simply couldn't improve his game. However, like many of us, he loved the sport and was unwilling to give up. One fine day, Stuart was out playing on the 5th hole, which was adjacent to a country road. Stuart stood over his shot, took a mighty swing, and missed completely. He addressed his shot again, swung, and found only air once again. Finally, on his third attempt, he barely made contact, and the ball rolled five feet forward. A man from the road had wandered onto the course to witness Stuart's futility and couldn't help but chuckle. The incensed golfer yelled at the bystander, "You'll have to leave! Only golfers are allowed on the golf course!" To which the man responded, "I won't say anything if you won't."

One way to determine the quality of a golf shot is to measure the amount of acceleration and deceleration . . . as the club goes back into the bag.

A salesman walks into a clubhouse and finds the head pro, who was quite busy. The salesman says, "I'd like to sell you some unique golf balls." To which the pro responds, "Sorry, we already have every kind of ball there." Undeterred, the salesman says, "You don't have these golf balls. They're amazing and you can't lose them." "Impossible," the pro responds. "What if you hit them into the water, or deep into the woods, or it gets dark and you can't see it?" "Not a problem," the salesman says, "If it goes into the water, it floats and then spins toward the shore. If it goes into the woods, it makes a beeping sound so you can find it. And in the dark it glows. I'm telling you, these balls are incredible. You simply can't lose them." "Okay. You've convinced me. I'll buy some," the head pro responds. "But I just have one question, since I've never heard of these balls before. Where did you get them?" The salesman smiled proudly and said, "I found them."

I'm a natural golfer. I've only been playing for a few weeks, and I can already throw my clubs as well as the golfers who have been playing for years.

An old man went to a new course and was paired with a much younger golfer. After the introductions were made, the younger man said, "Just for fun, do you want to put ten dollars on the round?" "That sounds like fun," came the reply from the elderly player. "How many shots do you need? I actually don't think I need any shots. I've been playing pretty well recently. My only issue is I struggle to get out of the traps." And as the men played, the younger man was truly impressed with his opponent. When they came to the 18th, the two men were all even. Both hit good drives, when the younger man put his second shot onto the green and the older man put his into the greenside bunker. The young man proceeded to two-putt while the older man holed out from the bunker to win. "Great shot," said the young man. "But I thought you said you struggled to get out of the bunkers?" "I do," came the reply from the trap. "Can you please give me a hand getting out of here?"

It always amazes me how a golfer who won't help out at all around the house will meticulously rake a sand trap, repair his ball marks, and replace their divots.

> *"Golf is the hardest game in the world to play, and the easiest to cheat at."*
> *—Dave Hill*

A young man who is an avid golfer was driving home from a work trip when he passed a course he had never played before. The golfer checked his watch and surmised that if he played quickly, he could squeeze in nine holes before dark. However, as he was about to get started, an old man shuffled toward the tee box and asked if he could join. Although the younger golfer was worried that the older player would slow him down, he reluctantly said, "Of course." To the young man's surprise, the older golfer played quickly. Although he didn't hit the ball very far, the senior player hit it straight and didn't waste any time. On the last hole, the junior player faced a tough shot when his ball landed behind a tree. The older golfer, who noticed the perilous predicament, said, "When I was your age, I would hit the ball right over that tree. The young man thanked him for the advice and gripped and ripped his shot, but unfortunately he watched in dismay as his ball rattled around in the branches and fell listlessly three feet away from where it started. The experienced golfer couldn't suppress a smile and stated, "You realize, of course, when I was your age that tree was only four feet tall."

What's Your Handicap?

A clearly arrogant golfer was at his club's annual dance when he started boasting to the prettiest woman there. "I'm a really terrific golfer," the man said. "What do you think my handicap is?" The woman, clearly not impressed, responded with, "Where would you like me to start?"

Most golfers have two handicaps—one when boasting about their game and one when money is on the line.

A rich man received a ransom note. It said that if he wanted to see his wife alive he needed to bring $20,000 to the 15th hole at 10 a.m. the next day. The man showed up with the money at 11:30, where he met a masked man who sneered, "You're late! Where the

hell have you been?" To which the man responded, "Hey, lay off. I have a twenty-four handicap."

There's one obscure direct correlation in golf. The higher the player's handicap, the more likely they are to give golf advice to others.

Marc had just finished his round at his club's handicap tournament and looked very upset. "What's the matter?" his friend asked. "Tough day on the course. You wouldn't believe it," Marc said. "They paired me up with Sean Sherman because we both have 17 handicaps. But Sean was actually a scratch golfer and shot a 71. I tell you . . . it's just so upsetting. I can't stand when people lie and cheat at golf." "Agreed," his friend responded. "That's really not fair." "You're telling me," Marc shot back. "I had to play like hell to beat him."

> *"On a recent survey, 80 percent of golfers admitted cheating. The other 20 percent lied."*
> *—Bruce Lansky*

For many golfers, their greatest handicap is the ability to add up their score correctly.

The Pro Said . . .

Golfer: "What's the best part of my game?" Teaching pro: "I'd say your short game . . . although that's off of the tee."

An old woman was growing bored with retirement and decided to take up golf. She went to the local club and signed up for a lesson. The pro showed the woman how to hold the club, swing, and then said, "Now just aim for the green and hit the ball. To the pro's surprise, the woman drove the ball right down the middle of the fairway, where it finally stopped just a few feet from the pin. "Now what do I do?" the woman asked. "Well you're supposed to hit the ball into the hole." The woman looked at the instructor and said, "Why didn't you tell me that earlier?"

Golfer: "Have you noticed any improvement since my last lesson?" Teaching pro: "Yes . . . it looks like you've lost a little weight."

A young avid golfer was paired up with three older players. Throughout the round, the senior players would often praise one another by saying, "Nice shot . . . that's a rider." The junior golfer didn't want to appear ignorant and ask about the expression, so he simply kept to himself. However, after the round, his curiosity got the best of him. He went to the head pro and said, "I've been playing golf for some time now, but I guess I'm not as educated as I thought. What is a 'rider'?" The pro laughed and said, "A rider is when you hit the ball far enough where you actually need to get in the cart and ride to it."

Golfer: "Do you think my golf game is improving?" Teaching pro: "Yes, I do. You're missing the ball much closer than you used to."

> "The greatest liar in the world is the golfer who claims he plays the game for merely exercise."
> —Tommy Bolt

A man was taking a lesson with his club pro. While on the range, the man's first shot was a wicked slice. "Why did that happen?" asked the man. "It was due to LOFT," the pro responded. His next shot was a severe duck hook. "What happened there?" the man asked again. The pro said, "That was also due to LOFT." On his third attempt, the man dribbled his shot three feet off of the tee. He looked expectantly at the professional, who said, "Yes . . . definitely due to a severe case of LOFT." Finally, the golfer asked, "What do you mean when you say 'LOFT'?" The professional looked down at his feet and said, "Lack of fine talent."

Golfer: "I keep striking behind the ball." Teaching pro: "That may be true, but in my opinion you're striking the course very well today."

Two men, who were both good golfers but not very bright, were out playing a round on a very foggy day. They could both make out the flag but couldn't see the green. They both hit what appeared to be decent shots, but they couldn't be sure. When they got to the green, however, they were pleasantly surprised. One ball had landed just inches from the hole, and the other one was actually in the cup. However, because both golfers had used a Titleist with the same number on it, they didn't know which ball belonged to each player. They decided to go see the club pro for a ruling. After explaining their stories, the club professional said, "Well first of all, kudos to both of you on playing such a fine shot. Now I just have one question: which one of you was playing the yellow ball?"

A novice golfer is playing with the club champion. At the end of the round, the club champ has tallied a three-under-par 69. "That was a terrific round" the novice gushes. "You really know your way around a golf course. What's your secret?" "It's really not that difficult," the proficient golfer responds modestly, "the holes are numbered."

Two golfers are talking when one says, "What do you think of the new golf pro?" "He seems like a good enough guy," answers his friend. "What do you think?" "In my opinion, he's a bit odd." "Why do you say that?" asks the second golfer. "He just tried to correct my stance," came the reply. The second golfer looked perplexed and says, "You realize that's he's only trying to help your golf game?" "Possibly," answers the first golfer, "but perhaps you should know that I was using the urinal at the time."

A congressman and his wife see the club pro in the parking lot getting out of his new Cadillac. Upon closer inspection, it appears that the pro is wearing a Rolex watch. "Can you believe that?" the congressman complains to his wife. "That club pro clearly makes more money than me." "Well, to be fair," his wife counters, "he is a better golfer than you."

> *"Golf has more rules than any other game because golf has more cheaters than any other game."*
> *—Bruce Lansky*

An expert golfer is playing with a hacker when they approach a 220-yard par 3. The skilled golfer takes out a three iron and lands his drive 15 feet past the hole, and then the spin takes it back to within 2 feet of the cup. His partner looks at him and asks, "How in the world did you make that ball back up?" The proficient golfer asks, "Do you ever use your three iron?" "Yes," comes the response. "All the time." And how far do you hit it?" "About 150 yards," replies the poor player. "The adept golfer simply smiles and says, "Then why in the world would you ever want your shot to back up?"

Two arrogant-looking men were in a clubhouse when they approached the local pro. "How can I help you?" the professional asked. "I'm interested in learning how to play this game like an expert," came the response. The instructor looked to his friend and asked, "Are you interested, as well?" "I don't need any more help," came the reply. "I had my lesson yesterday."

A crotchety old golfer was set to tee off when he saw a young boy teeing off right before him. Worried that the young lad might hold him up, he went to the head pro and said, "That boy looks like he's six years old." To which the pro responded, "It's probably better that way. He likely can't count past ten."

Perry went out with the club pro for a round. When they finished and were on their way back to the clubhouse, Perry asked, "What do you think of my game?" The pro thought for a minute and replied "Honestly, I would shorten your clubs by two inches." "Do you really think that would improve my game?" the man asked excitedly. "Not really," said the pro, "But it will help to fit them into the trash can."

Homer was not considered a very bright man, but he loved the game of golf and was always trying to buy himself a better game. One day he went into the clubhouse and asked the pro if he could recommend anything that might improve his score. "Believe it or not" the professional said, "we actually have new clubs that I think could cut your handicap in half." "Terrific," Homer replied, "I'll take two sets."

Twosomes & Foursomes

Two friends invited their priest to play a round of golf. Although he wasn't very good, the priest accepted the invitation. When they got to the course, a fourth player joined them. In an attempt to put him at ease, the priest insisted that he be introduced by his first name. On the 18th hole, the fourth player asked the priest what he did for a living, at which point he admitted that he was part of the clergy. "I knew it!" the man exclaimed. "How did you know?" the priest asked. "Because anyone who plays golf that poorly and doesn't swear has got to be a man of God."

> *"Golf combines two favorite American pastimes: taking long walks and hitting things with a stick."*
> —P.J. O'Rourke

Moses and Jesus are playing a round in heaven. On the 18th, Jesus has a particularly difficult shot. He lines it up, takes a mighty swing, and the ball explodes from his club. Moses and Jesus watch as the ball bounces off three different trees, then hits a rock, lands softly on the green, and trickles into the hole. Moses looks at Jesus and says, "Nice shot. But are we going to play golf or goof around?"

Two fur traders went out for a round of golf. They wanted to make it exciting, so they decided to play a skins match.

A recently married man is playing golf with his conservative father-in-law. Trying to impressive his new wife's father, he is on his best behavior. However, after a string of bad shots, he loses his temper and swears loudly. The father-in-law, clearly unhappy, says, "I've noticed that the best golfers rarely use profanity." "That may be true," the still-upset younger man replied. "But what the hell do they have to be upset about?"

Golfer one: "Want to play golf today?" Golfer two: "Sorry, the doctor told me I can't play." Golfer one: "Oh, he's seen you play, as well."

The best golf partner is one that is just a little bit more lousy than you.

Golfer number one: "Has your swing changed much over the years?" Golfer number two: "It hasn't changed much, but it has definitely changed often."

> *"Don't play too much golf. Two rounds a day are plenty."*
> *—Harry Vardon*

Two golfers were introducing themselves to each other on the first tee when one golfer said, "How do you feel about a lot of screaming and foul language?" "It doesn't bother me at all," came the reply. "Great," said the first golfer. "Then would you please call my wife before we get started and let her know I'm playing golf again today?"

My buddy asked me, "Why don't you play golf with Frank anymore? You two used to play together all of the time." I looked him square in the eye and said, "Let me ask you a question. Would you play with a guy who constantly lies and cheats on nearly every hole?" "I definitely would not," my friend responded. "Well, neither would Frank."

A player stood on the 18th tee for what seemed like forever. He was practicing his swing, checking the wind, measuring the distance, and driving his partner crazy. Finally, his comrade said, "Come on, already. What's taking so long? Hit the ball already." The golfer took a step back and said, "My wife is in the clubhouse watching me. This shot needs to be perfect." "Forget about it," his

exasperated partner said. "There is no way you'll be able to hit her from here."

Two golfers were discussing their day on the course when the first golfer said, "I played a World War II round today." "What's a World War II round?" the second golfer inquired. "I was out in '39 and home in '45," came the response. "Interesting" responded the second golfer. "Then I guess I played a Civil War round . . . out in '61 and home in '65."

Two golfers are standing on a long par five when the first golfer says, "I'll bet you five dollars that I can reach the green with my drive." "You're on," replies the second golfer, already counting his money. The first man gets up and takes a mighty swipe. The ball goes off course and lands in the adjoining road, where it bounces for two hundred yards before hitting the tire of a moving vehicle and getting knocked onto the green. "That was incredible," the second man says. "How in the world did you do that?" "Well, it helps if you know the bus schedule."

Two old friends were mediocre golfers, but they played religiously. Rain or shine, in good and bad weather, they rarely missed their daily game. However, on one particularly frustrating day, when they were both having terrible rounds, one friend turned to the other and said, "Remind me why we put ourselves through this agony." "Isn't it obvious?" the second friend said. "We've both got spouses at home."

> *"'Play it as it lies' is one of the fundamental dictates of golf. The other is 'Wear it if it clashes.'"*
> *—Henry Beard*

Golfer #1: "Are you bad at golf?" Golfer #2: "I'm terrible." Golfer #1: "Join the club."

George and Jerry have been best friends and golfing partners for years. They made a pact that the first to die would let the other know if there was golf in heaven. Sure enough, after George passed away, true to his word he came to Jerry in a vision and said, "Jerry, I have good news and bad news." "What's the good news?" Jerry asked excitedly. "There's golf in heaven," his friend replied. "Then what's the bad news?" Jerry asked. "We're teeing off together on Tuesday."

Three members of a golf group were arguing while the fourth member lay dead on the course. When the club official approached them and asked what happened, the outraged golfer said, "My partner had a stroke, and these idiots are trying to add it to my score."

Two really old golfers are on the first tee when the first says to the second, "How is your eyesight?" "For a man of my age, it's surprisingly good," says the second man. "Excellent," says the first man. "Would you mind watching my drive? I love playing golf, but my vision is not what it used to be." "I'm happy to be helpful," comes the reply. The first golfer then proceeds to rip his drive and says, "Did you see my drive?" "I sure did," the second man says with pride. "So where is it?" The second golfer thinks for a few seconds, then sheepishly responds, "I don't remember."

Four elderly friends were out golfing when the first said, "It seems as if these holes are getting longer every year." "It also seems like the sand traps are getting bigger, as well," said the second man. The third golfer agreed, saying, "Not only that, but is it just me or are the hills getting steeper, as well?" "Agreed," said the fourth and final friend. "However, we should be thankful that at least we're all still on the top side of the grass."

Ellen and Mary are playing a round when they come to the 5th tee, which is overlooking a lake. Ellen proceeds to hit her drive right into the middle of the drink. She then realizes that she was out of balls and asks Mary for one. Mary obliges, and Ellen then hits her next shot into the water, as well. Mary then gives her friend one, two, three more golf balls, but the outcome is the same. Finally, when Ellen asks for yet another ball, Mary says, "Ellen, these balls are expensive." To which Ellen responds, "If you can't afford to play golf, then you should pick up a less expensive sport."

"You can't call it a sport. You don't run, jump, you don't shoot, you don't pass. All you have to do is buy some clothes that don't match."
—Steve Sax

Four old golfers had been playing together for years. While they all enjoyed the camaraderie, they took the game very seriously. So on one glorious day, when Fred walked off of the course to the side of the road and tipped his cap to a passing funeral procession, the players were somewhat surprised. When Fred came back to hit his next shot, one of the other players had to comment on the unusual occurrence. "Fred," he began, "that was a very nice gesture." As Fred began his backswing, he retorted, "It's the least I could do. I mean, we were married for 50 years."

Two old friends meet after years of separation. "How have you been?" asks the first friend. "How has retirement been treating you?" "All is well," replies the second. "I've really been enjoying all of my free time. I actually took up golf." "Wow, that's terrific," offers the first friend. "Are you any good?" "I'm actually a scratch golfer." "Incredible. And you've only been playing for a short amount of time. That's really impressive." "Not really," answers the friend modestly. "It's just that every time I hit the ball, I scratch my head and wonder why I started playing golf in the first place."

A doctor, an accountant, and a lawyer are all playing golf on a beautiful, sunny day. Unfortunately, the foursome in front of them is playing incredibly slowly. The three players continue to complain about the pace of play throughout the round. Finally, when they walk off the course and into the clubhouse, they are infuriated. As they complain to the head pro, he calmly informs them that the foursome is made up of blind golfers who were invited to the club as part of a charity exhibition. The doctor, immediately contrite, says, "Wow, I feel terrible, I'd like to donate $500 to the charity." The accountant says, "I feel terrible, as well. I'd like to donate $1,000." The lawyer looks pensive and says, "You're telling me those golfers are blind?" "That's right," says the pro. "Then why not just have them play at night?"

Two old friends were involved in a match-play event when they found themselves all-square on the 18th. The first friend hit his shot onto a cart path and stated, "I guess I should get a drop." "Definitely not," came the reply. "We play our shots where they lie." So the first man dropped his friend off at his ball and took the cart to the path. He took a few practice swings, causing sparks to fly. Finally, he swatted the ball from the path, and incredibly it landed just a couple of feet from the pin. "Nice shot," conceded the second golfer. "What club did you use?" "Your five iron."

Golf is a strange sport. You start with three friends, play a game together for several hours, and end with three enemies.

A man is playing with his wife when he finds his ball in a perilous position sitting behind two large trees with a narrow opening between them. The man's wife encourages him to try and shoot the ball between the narrow opening. "I'll never make that shot," the man says. "It's too narrow. But when the woman insists, he decides to go for it. Unfortunately, the ball strikes one of the trees, shoots directly back, and hits his wife in the head, killing her instantly. A week later the man is back out on the course with an acquaintance when he finds himself in the exact same place behind the two large trees. The man encourages him to go for it again, when the widower says, "I can't take that risk. You know what happened last time, don't you?" The acquaintance replies with, "No, I don't. What happened?" "I made a triple bogey."

> *"I learned one thing from jumping motorcycles that was of great value on the golf course, the putting green especially. Whatever you do, don't come up short."*
> *—Evel Knievel*

Golfer #1: "What did you get on your last hole?" Golfer #2: "Depressed."

Diane and Phyllis were about to start their round when Phyllis noticed that Diane had a new set of clubs. "Nice clubs," Phyllis said. "How do you like them?" "They're great," replied Diane. "Have they helped your game?" "They've helped a lot," Diane gushed. "I never knew I could hit with so much power. I mean, they've added 20 yards to my hooks, 30 yards to my slices, and my divots are bigger than ever!"

The Short Game

G olf is 90 percent mental. That's why most golfers are crazy.

What is a golfer's biggest fear? The bogeyman.

Golf is a game that is 10 percent mental and 90 percent mental.

What does a golfer like to hear from their significant other? Talk "birdie" to me.

> *"These greens are so fast I have to hold my putter over the ball and hit it with the shadow."*
> —Sam Snead

The game of golf is like taking a beautiful five-mile walk with lots of disappointments sprinkled in.

What's the difference between a pro and amateur golfer? The amateur retires to play more golf.

Why couldn't Jack Nicklaus listen to music? Because he broke all of the records.

It's not whether you win or lose at golf that counts, it's whether I win or lose.

It's a lot easier to hit a fairway when you're open to choosing from several of them.

Old Golfer: "I'm not over the hill. I'm simply playing the back nine."

> *"Putting allows the touchy golfer two to four opportunities to blow a gasket in the short space of two to forty feet."*
> *—Tommy Bolt*

"Sweetheart. Tell me about that amazing golf shot you hit again. I'm having trouble falling asleep."

"I wish I could play my regular game . . . if just one time."

Golf was once a sport only for the rich. But now that this great game has come to the masses, there are plenty of poor players, as well.

What's a surefire way to find water on Mars? Send a golfer up there to play a round.

A bad day at golf sure beats a good day at work.

There is no such thing in golf as a shot so easy that it can't be screwed up.

> *"Even when times were good, I realized that my earning power as a golf professional depended on too many ifs and putts."*
> —*Gene Sarazen*

If you get caught in a lightning storm, hold up your one iron, because even the Good Lord can't hit a one iron.

Why do true golfers always avoid pie whenever possible? Because they are worried that they might get a slice.

The golfer estimated that his shot landed about 25 yards left of the fairway. Of course, that was just a rough estimate.

Golf is actually a pretty easy game. It's just hard to play.

Golf is a game where the balls lie poorly and the players lie well.

If the point of golf is to hit the ball as few times as possible, if I don't play at all, do I win?

> *"Talking to a golf ball won't do you any good, unless you do it while your opponent is teeing off."*
> *—Bruce Lansky*

A decent shot on the 18th hole has stopped many golfers from giving up the game.

Golfers who claim a shank is close to a perfect shot have never hit two good shots in a row.

I don't mind shooting in the 130s. The way I see it, I'm getting more for my money.

Why do clergy have a distinct advantage while playing golf? They have a lot of practice keeping their heads down.

Why is the worst golfer at the club known as "The James Bond of Golf?" Because after every hole he says, "Oh, oh, seven."

What are the three worst words you can hear on the golf course? You're still away.

> *"There are three things in the world that he held in the smallest esteem—slugs, poets and caddies with hiccups."*
> —P.G. Wodehouse

Why is it that most golfers rarely make the same mistakes twice? Because they seldom do anything the same way twice in golf.

The easiest way to improve at golf is to play with poorer playing partners.

What is the perfect golf shot called? A fluke.

My wife thinks I took up golf just so I could be useless on weekends, too.

How does golf differ from nuclear physics? Golf is much more complicated.

> *"A Major golf tournament is 40,000 sadists watching 144 masochists."*
> *—Thomas Boswe*

What do golfers and children have in common? They can't count past five.

Why are computers so good at golf? Because they have hard drives.

How does a spouse keep their avid golfing better half at home? By hiding their clubs.

The only difference between a practice swing and a whiff is that no one ever wants to give up the game after a practice swing.

What's the best part of the golf course to be on? The top part.

Why are golf balls similar to eggs? Because they're white, normally sold by the dozen, and every week you need to buy more of them.

> *"The game of golf is an enigma wrapped in a mystery impaled on a conundrum."*
> *—Peter Alliss*

What do the worst drivers and the worst golfers have in common? They should both wear a sign that says, "How's My Driving?"

My golf game is so pathetic that I recently had to regrip my ball retriever.

What do you call 50 golfers holding hands on a stone beach? The Pebble Beach Golf Links.

Golf is a game that was created by the Good Lord to punish those who retire too early.

How is golf like a man who is down on his luck? You're constantly getting out of one hole only to find yourself in another.

"Professional golf is the only sport where, if you win twenty percent of the time, you're the best."
—Jack Nicklaus

What's the real reason that golf pros tell you to keep your head down during a lesson? So you can't see them laughing.

No matter how badly you play golf, you can always get worse.

Despite what many people think, most golfers play an honest game. Of course, that's only when you're watching them closely.

What's the difference between a golf ball and directions? Most men will ask for help finding a golf ball.

Why is golf so frustrating? Could it be because it was invented by the same people who think good music comes out of a bagpipe?

The problem with most golfers is they stand way too close to the ball after they hit it.

> *"In no other sport must the spectator move."*
> —John Updike

Only a golfer would hire someone to mow their lawn so they had the time to get some exercise on the golf course.

An exclusive golf club is the kind of place where you would have blackballed most of the members if you had gotten in first.

The only two good drives many golfers have is the trip to and from the course.

My golf partner is so frustrating. He makes all sorts of promises on the course but never follows through.

If you think that meeting new people is difficult, just try picking up the wrong ball on a golf course.

Golf is very similar to paying your taxes. You strive for the green but eventually come out in the hole.

> *"Golf is a day spent in a round of*
> *strenuous idleness."*
> *—William Wordsworth*

The only thing that causes more lying than golf is paying your taxes.

How do golfers differ from most people? Golfers are more likely to reach 100.

What's the difference between golf and other sports? It takes at least 50 years to be this bad at golf.

Why was Darth Vader a good golfer? Because the Fours were with him.

Golf is the only sport where the slowest players are in the front, whereas the fastest have to play from behind.

Golf is a great game to pick up when you are too out of shape to play softball.

> *"Golf's three ugliest words:*
> *still your shot."*
> *—Dave Marr*

Why do good golfers always carry two pairs of pants? In case they get a hole in one.

For most golfers, the best wood in their bag is the pencil.

Marital Bliss

Elderly woman: "When I die I want to be buried on a golf course so I can ensure that my husband will visit me."

A man was about to tee off when a woman came running up to the tee box. "How could you?" she cried. "How could you leave me at the altar to play golf?" To which the golfer calmly replied, "I don't know why you're getting so bent out of shape. I specifically told you only if it rained."

A man and his wife have been arguing about the amount of golf he plays. The arguments had been going on for weeks when one day, the woman comes home and finds the man in bed with his golf clubs. "What in the world are you doing?" the woman asked. "Well, you said I had to choose."

A couple is about to get married when the groom says to his soon-to-be bride, "Honey, I love you, and I want to be completely honest with you. I'm an absolute golf fanatic. And I play, eat, drink, sleep, and think about golf 24 hours a day, seven days a week. "Well, since we're being honest" the future wife says, "I'm actually a hooker." "That's okay, sweetheart," the groom says with empathy. "Just make sure to keep your left arm straight and your head down."

> *"Golf is a game of expletives not deleted."*
> *—Dr. Irving Gladstone*

A golfer approached a woman as she walked out of the clubhouse and said, "Do you pay a high price to play golf here?" "I will today," she replied. "I told my husband I was taking a quick run to the grocery store and that I'd be home in 20 minutes."

Wife: "You're obsessed with golf." Husband: "Do you think it's driving a wedge between us?"

A newly married couple was having dinner when the wife said, "Now that we're married, I think we need to spend some quality time together. Therefore, I think you should play less golf." "You're beginning to sound a lot like my ex-wife," the husband answered. "I didn't know you were previously married," his surprised wife said. "I wasn't," came the dry reply.

Woman one: "I just got a new set of golf clubs for my husband." Woman two: "Great trade!"

A man and his wife are arguing about how much golf he plays. "You're out on that course every day, rain or shine, you're neglecting your family, and you're not even that good." "What are you talking about?" the man retorts. "There are many people who are worse at golf than me." "That may be true," his wife concedes, "although most of them are people who have never picked up a club."

A man and his soon-to-be wife are about to get married. They are standing at the church with the glowing bride dressed in white and the groom-to-be in his finest suit. As the ceremony is about to begin, the bride notices the groom's golf clubs in the corner of the church. "Why are you clubs here?" the perplexed woman asks. The man, somewhat stunned, replies, "This isn't going to take all day, is it?"

> *"Golf is like life in a lot of ways. All the biggest wounds are self-inflicted."*
> *—Bill Clinton*

A wife is getting upset with her husband for neglecting her and spending too much time playing and thinking about golf. The couple begins to argue, and finally the woman says, "I bet you don't even remember the day we got engaged." "Well, that just goes to show you how very wrong you are. I remember it vividly," the man shoots back. "It was the last time I shot even par."

A married couple is out on the course when out of nowhere the husband asks,

"Babe, if I die will you marry again?"

Wife: "Of course not."

Husband: "I think you should."

Wife: "Fine, I probably will"

Husband: "Will you let him sleep in our bed?"

Wife: "Probably."

Husband: "Would you let him use my golf clubs?"

Wife: "Of course not, he's left-handed."

The Lamaze class was full of pregnant women and their partners. When the class was coming to an end, the instructor said, "Remember ladies, exercise is good for you. Don't forget to take a walk as often as possible. And gentlemen, it wouldn't be a bad

idea for you to go walking with your partners. Are there any ques-
tions?" A hand went up from the back of the room. "Yes," replied the
instructor. "Is it okay if my wife carries a golf bag while we walk?"

Is There a Doctor in the House?

A woman is at the club with her family when she notices her baby swallowing her golf tees. She immediately calls her pediatrician and screams, "My child just ingested my golf tees." The concerned doctor says, "Don't worry. I'll be there at once." "What should I do until you get here, doctor?" the worried woman asks. "Practice your short game."

John was leaving work early again to play golf, and his boss had had enough. "You're leaving early again to go to the course?" the frustrated boss asked. "I'm just following my doctor's orders," John replied. "Do you think I'm an idiot?" the boss shot back. "No, it's true. My doctor told me to get some iron every day."

Where can you always find at least 100 doctors at the same place? At the golf course.

> *"I'm not feeling very well. I need a doctor immediately. Ring the nearest golf course."*
> *—Groucho Marx*

My doctor told me to play 18 holes a day. After a frustrating couple of weeks on the course, I ended up buying a harmonica.

A dentist who loved to play golf decided to play hooky and cancel all of his appointments for the day. He therefore left the following coy message on his work answering machine: Thank you for calling. Unfortunately, the dentist is very busy today, as he has 18 patients scheduled. Please call back tomorrow.

A golfer with an iron deficiency went to see his doctor and was informed that he was still not out of the woods.

Why is a golf course the safest place to be? Because if you have a heart attack, there's always going to be a doctor nearby.

For the Love of the Game

A die-hard golfer's diet involves living on the greens as much as possible.

> "Playing the game I have learned the meaning of humility. It has given me an understanding of futility of the human effort."
> —Abba Eban

A nervous golfer was pacing back and forth in a hospital looking quite nervous. When the nurse inquired, he told her that a ball had been hit awry and ended up in the throat of the man in surgery. The nurse then asked, "Is the patient a relative of yours? Is that why you're so nervous?" "Actually," the man said, "I'm just hoping to get my ball back."

Why did Tarzan love to play golf? Because he enjoyed working on his swing.

Two new golfers are discussing their newfound love of the sport when the first golfer says, "I found a new helpful trick. It's important to study the marker next to the tee shot before you hit." "Why is that?" asks his friend. "Does it help you with choosing the correct club?" "Not really," comes the reply, "but it does help me play the correct hole."

What does a golfing fanatic think walking down the green is? A romantic walk.

Three old friends met at their high school reunion. The first man said, "I have four kids. One more and I could have a basketball team." The second man says, "That's nothing. I have 10 kids. One more I'll have enough for a football team." The third man laughed and said, "I have you both beat. I have seventeen kids. One more and I'll have a golf course."

You know you're addicted to golf when you quit the game forever . . . every weekend.

> *"It's easy to see golf not as a game at all but as some whey-faced, nineteenth-century Presbyterian minister's fever dream of exorcism achieved through ritual and self-mortification."*
> *—Bruce McCall*

After a lovely church service, a new couple approached the pastor. The wife introduced herself and said, "We'd like to become members of your church." To which the clergyman replied, "That's wonderful." And then, addressing his comments to the husband, asked, "And where did you previously attend?" The man, with tears in his eyes, responded, "The local golf course."

It's easier to get up at 6 a.m. to play golf than it is to wake up at 10 a.m. to mow the lawn.

A golfer called his friend and was very upset. "I can't believe it," the despondent man said, "my wife of 30 years left me for my golf partner." His sympathetic friend replied, "Oh no, that's terrible. But don't worry, there are a lot of other women out there. You'll surely find love again." "Who's worried about her?" said the scorned man. "I was talking about my playing partner. He was the only guy I could ever beat."

You know you're addicted to golf when you miss the ball but still believe it was a solid swing.

When the police arrived at Charlie's house, they found his wife dead on the kitchen floor. There was a bloody golf club lying next to her body. The police officer asked, "Did you kill this woman?" "Yes, I did," Charlie answered matter-of-factly. "It appears that you hit her in the head nine times with this five iron. Is that accurate?" "Yes," Charlie answered honestly. "But if you could put me down for a five, I would appreciate it."

McDermott and McDuff were sitting in front of a crackling fire on a freezing day in the outskirts of Glasgow, where the snow was coming down hard. With their frozen beards thawing in front of the fire, they sipped their pints of beer as they contemplated their surroundings. Finally, McDermott stated, "That was quite a round of golf." McDuff looked up from his drink and replied, "Same time next week?" "Aye," McDermott retorted, "weather permitting."

> *"Golf, like the measles, should be caught young, for if postponed to riper years the results may be serious."*
> —*P.G. Wodehouse*

One pathetic golfer says to the other, "We've only played 4 holes and have already hit our ages."

Two friends are out at a club when a woman walks past them wearing a leather dress. The first man looks to the wingman and says, "How sexy is that?" The second man looks at the first man and says, "Wow, I didn't know the look of a leather dress turned you on." "It's not the look. It's actually the smell." "Really?" said his friend, "What is it about the smell that you like?" The man smiles sheepishly and replies, "It smells just like a new golf glove."

Golf is a very frustrating game! Don't believe me? Yesterday I was just three strokes away from a hole in one.

A man was attempting to book a round of golf at an exclusive club but wasn't having any luck. "I'm sorry," the secretary explained, "we simply don't have any tee times today." The man, undaunted, said, "Let me ask you a question. What if the president wanted to play a round today? Would you be able to find him a tee time?"

"Well, of course," responded the secretary. The man then replied, "I happen to know he's tied up today, so I'll take his tee time."

No matter how bad you are at golf, one incredibly lucky hole in one can keep you playing for the rest of your life.

A recently retired business executive is discussing his new life with his friend. "How is your retirement?" the friend asks. "It's terrific," the retiree says. "The only downside is I've had to give up skiing." Why is that?" his friend asks, "Are you afraid of getting hurt?" "I am now," he responded. "You see, in the past, if I broke my ankle, I could still work . . . no big deal. But now, even the slightest injury while skiing could truly affect my golf game . . . it's just not worth the risk."

> *"When Nicklaus plays well, he wins. When he plays badly, he finishes second. When he plays terribly, he finishes third."*
> *—Johnny Miller*

You know you're addicted to golf when your goal is to shoot your age but a more realistic goal would be to shoot your weight.

Moe and Joe were playing a delightful round when Moe hit an errant drive. The drive was so far off track that it actually struck another golfer in the head on an adjoining hole. Moe and Joe rushed to the wounded player and found him lying on the course unconscious. "Oh my God," yelled Moe. "What should we do?" "Well, definitely don't move him," Joe replied. "If we leave him in place, he will be deemed an immovable obstruction, and you can either play the ball as it lies or take a two-club-length drop."

In a primitive society, when people beat the grounds with clubs, it was considered witchcraft. In today's modern world, it's called golf.

A man and his wife entered a dentist's office. The man said, "I'm in hurry. I have a tee time in 30 minutes. There's no time for anesthesia. Just pull the tooth so I can make my golf game." The dentist looked at the man with awe and said, "Are you sure? It's really going to hurt without an anesthetic." "I don't care," the man snapped. "We're talking about golf here." "Ok," said the dentist, "which tooth is it?" The man turned to his wife and said, "Open your mouth, sweetheart, and show the dentist which tooth hurts."

You know you're addicted to golf when you understand that there's more to life than golf but you're not interested in finding out what that is.

Mary Sue was an avid golfer. She looked forward to her weekly game with the enthusiasm of a six-year-old on Christmas morning. However, one day, she came home looking haggard. Her husband,

who was obviously concerned, asked what happened. "It was terrible," Mary Sue responded. "On the fifth hole, Ellen had a heart attack and died instantly. "That's awful!" her husband empathized. "You're telling me," Mary Sue said as she lay down on the sofa. "For the rest of the round it was hit the ball, drag Ellen. Hit the ball, drag Ellen. It was exhausting!"

> *"Bob Hope has a beautiful short game. Unfortunately, it's off the tee."*
> *—Jimmy Demaret*

An avid golfer is standing on an elevated tee overlooking a river when he comments to his friend, "Look at those morons fishing like that in the rain."

As George Smith's neighbor approached his house, George was already fuming. *He's always trying to borrow something, and I'm sick of it,* George thought. *I'm not going to let him get away with it this time.* When the neighbor knocked on George's door, he was ready. "Howdy George," the neighbor began, "I was wondering if I could borrow your lawn mower?" "Sorry, neighbor, but as you can see I have a very big lawn, and I'll be using it all day." "In that case," the crafty neighbor said, "Do you mind if I borrow your golf clubs? You obviously won't be needing them."

One married avid golfer to another: "It seems to me that the hardest thing about golf is convincing your spouse to let you out of the house every day to play."

Like many golf enthusiasts, Alice was always trying to buy herself a better golf game. She invested lots of her hard-earned money into lessons, clothes, and of course her equipment. The pro shop staff knew her well and always tried to keep her happy, as their commissions depended on it. So after Alice bought the most expensive clubs in the store, the assistant who sold them to her was eager to hear about her first round with her new weapons. "Alice," the employee asked, "how was your round?" "It was great!" Alice retorted with sarcasm spewing. "I can throw these clubs 20 yards farther than my previous ones."

When you get to the point that you love golf so much that you're happy to also play in the snow, rain, and even in a hurricane, life as you know it is in serious peril.

A husband and wife were talking about their son when the wife said, "Honey, Junior's getting older. I think it's time to have the important talk with him." "Enough said," the man replied. "I was thinking the same thing." So the father sat his son down and said, "Young man, there are going to be times in your life when you have strange feelings that you've never had before. You might notice that your palms are getting sweaty and that your heart seems to be pounding out of your chest." As the boy listened intently, he finally asked, "Is it anything to worry about?" "Not at all," his father assured him. "It's all perfectly normal. It's simply called golf."

> *"I owe everything to golf. Where else could a guy with an IQ like mine make this much money?"*
> —Hubert Green

At first, taking up golf is a good way to take your mind off of your work. However, soon thereafter you'll need to dive back into work to take your mind off of golf.

As the archeologists continued to uncover the lost city in the jungle, the excitement was palpable. And when they saw what appeared to be wide areas with circular holes spaced evenly throughout the lengthy terrain, it became evident that an ancient golf course was being uncovered. The question then became "Why would this ancient civilization give up the game only to have it reappear centuries later?" The head archeologist decided that the only possibility of an answer was to enlist the assistance of the chief local tribesman. When posed with the head-scratching question, the chief said, "I believe I have the answer to your question." "Please . . . enlighten us." "Well it's obvious, isn't it?" the chief said knowingly. "They clearly couldn't afford the green fees."

It takes longer to get good at golf than it does to learn how to perform brain surgery. On the other hand, you don't get to drink beer, ride in a cart, and tell bad jokes while in surgery.

An avid golfer passed away and went up to Heaven. When he approached the Pearly Gates, he asked St. Peter, "Before I come in, can I see the golf course?" Although St. Peter had never heard this request before, he acquiesced. However, when the man saw the course, he was somewhat disappointed, as it wasn't what he had hoped for. Just then, the Devil came around the corner and offered to show the man the course in Hell. Although somewhat reluctant, the man agreed. However, once they arrived, the Devil showed the man the most beautiful course he had ever seen. "You've convinced me," said the man. "I'll stay." "Terrific," said the devil. "Please let me know where the golf clubs are," the man said. But the devil just roared with laughter and said, "We don't have any golf clubs in Hell."

What's the difference between bad golfers and bad skydivers? When listening to most bad golfers, you're likely to first hear "Whack" followed by "Ugh," whereas when listening to most poor skydivers, you're likely to first hear "Ugh" followed by "Whack."

The 19th Hole

W here is the only place you're allowed to drink after you drive? The 19th hole.

> "Show me a man with a great golf game, and I'll show you a man who has been neglecting something."
> —John F. Kennedy

Two golfers are at the 19th hole having a drink after their respective rounds when one golfer says, "You're not going to believe this, but I scored a 12 on the par-3 17th hole. "Wow!" says the second golfer. "How in the world did that happen?" The first golfer smiles and says, "I holed out from the greenside bunker."

A golfer is drowning his sorrows at the 19th hole. The bartender approaches the man and says, "Tough round?" "I actually had the best round of my life," the man says with tears in his eyes. "Then why so glum?" "My wife said that I play too much golf and if I don't cut way back she's going to leave me." "What are you going to do?" the sympathetic bartender asks. "I'm really going to miss her."

Golf is a strange game. Don't believe me? You need to hit down to make the ball go up. When you swing left, the ball goes right. The lowest score wins. And the winner has to buy the drinks.

A 75-year-old wealthy man shows up to the golf course with a beautiful, much younger woman on his arm. His friends are more than curious. When they get their friend alone, they ask, "Is that your girlfriend?" "Actually, she's now my wife," the proud man says. "How in the world did you get a woman like that to marry you?" the friends inquire. "It was easy. I simply lied about my age." "Oh, we get it," the friends say with knowing smiles. "Did you tell her you were 50?" "No," came the reply. "90."

A well-known hacker is full of glee while speaking with his friend at the clubhouse. "What's got you in such a good mood?" his comrade asks. "I finally broke 90!" the happy man boasts. "Wow, good for you. No wonder why you're in such a good mood." "Thank you,"

the man says happily. I'm really so proud of myself that I had to skip the back nine and come right to the 19th hole to celebrate . . . drinks are on me!"

The Long Drive Home

One of the truest statements in all of sports goes as follows: There is nothing better than a long walk with a putter in your hand. Unfortunately, for most of us weekend warriors, these moments are few and far between. But don't despair, because as every golfer who has ever hacked through a round knows all too well, it only takes that one magical shot to keep you coming back and yearning for more. In the meantime, don't forget to laugh your frustration away. If you ever need a pick-me-up, there's a chuckle waiting nearby in *Golf Jokes*.